Sergeant York's Own Story

Sam K. Cowan

Kessinger Publishing's Rare Reprints

Thousands of Scarce and Hard-to-Find Books on These and other Subjects!

- Americana
- Ancient Mysteries
- Animals
- Anthropology
- Architecture
- Arts
- Astrology
- Bibliographies
- Biographies & Memoirs
- Body, Mind & Spirit
- Business & Investing
- Children & Young Adult
- Collectibles
- Comparative Religions
- Crafts & Hobbies
- Earth Sciences
- Education
- Ephemera
- Fiction
- Folklore
- Geography
- Health & Diet
- History
- Hobbies & Leisure
- Humor
- Illustrated Books
- Language & Culture
- Law
- Life Sciences
- Literature
- Medicine & Pharmacy
- Metaphysical
- Music
- Mystery & Crime
- Mythology
- Natural History
- Outdoor & Nature
- Philosophy
- Poetry
- Political Science
- Science
- Psychiatry & Psychology
- Reference
- Religion & Spiritualism
- Rhetoric
- Sacred Books
- Science Fiction
- Science & Technology
- Self-Help
- Social Sciences
- Symbolism
- Theatre & Drama
- Theology
- Travel & Explorations
- War & Military
- Women
- Yoga
- *Plus Much More!*

**We kindly invite you to view our catalog list at:
http://www.kessinger.net**

VI

*SERGEANT
YORK'S
OWN STORY*

VI

Sergeant York's Own Story

WHEN Alvin went to war he carried with him a small, red, cloth-covered memorandum book, which was to be his diary. He knew that beyond the mountains that encircled his home there was a world that would be new to him. He kept the little volume—now with broken-back and worn—constantly with him, and he wrote in it while in camp, on shipboard and in the trenches in France. It was in his pocket while he fought the German machine gun battalion in the Forest of Argonne.

The book with its records was intended for no eyes but his own. Yet painstaking, using ink, he had headed the volume: "A History of places where I have been."

As a whole, the volume would be unintelligible to a reader, for while it records the things he wished to remember of his camp-life, the trip through England, his stay in France, and tells in order the "places he had been," it is made up of swift-moving notes that enter into no explanatory details. But to him the notations could—even in the evening of his life—revive the chain of incidents in memory. His handling of his diary is typical of his mind and his methods.

To him details are essential, but when they are done carefully and thoroughly their functions are performed and thereafter they are uninteresting. They are but the steps that must be taken to walk a given distance. His mind instead dwells upon the object of the walk.

When he left his home at Pall Mall he reported to the local recruiting station at Jamestown, the county seat. He was sent to Camp Gordon near Atlanta, Ga., and reached there the night of November 16, 1917. His diary runs:

"I was placed in the 21st training battalion. Then I was called the first morning of my army life to police up in the yard all the old cigarette butts and I thought that was pretty hard as I didn't smoke. But I did it just the same."

His history tells in one sentence, of months of his experience in training with the "awkward squad" and of his regimental assignment:

"I stayed there and done squads right and squads left until the first of February, 1918, and then I was sent to Company G, 328 Inf. 82nd Div."

This was the "All America" Division, made up of selected men from every state in the Union and in its ranks were the descendants of men who came from every nation that composed the Allies that were fighting Germany.

In his notes Alvin records temptations that came to him while at Camp Gordon:

"Well they gave me a gun and, oh my! that old gun was just full of grease, and I had to clean that old gun for inspection. So I had a hard time to get that old gun clean, and oh, those were trying hours for a boy like me trying to live for God and do his blessed will. . . . Then the Lord would help me to bear my hard tasks.

"So there I was. I was the homesickest boy you ever seen."

When he entered the army Alvin York stood six feet in the clear. There were but few in camp physically his equal. In any crowd of men he drew attention. The huge muscles of his body glided lithely over each other. He had been swinging with long, firm strides up the mountainsides. His arms

and shoulders had developed by lifting hay-
ladened pitchforks in the fields and in the
swing of the sledge in his father's black-
smith's shop. The military training coordi-
nated these muscles and he moved among
the men a commanding figure, whose quiet
reserve power seemed never fully called into
action by the arduous duties of the soldier.

The strength of his mind, the brain force
he possessed were yet to be recognized and
tested. And even to-day, with all the experi-
ences he has had and the advancement he
has made, that force is not yet measured. It
is in the years of the future that the real
mission of Sergeant York will be told.

He came out of the mountains of Tennessee with an education equal to that of a child
of eight or nine years of age, with no experience in the world beyond the primitive,
wholesome life of his mountain community,
with but little knowledge of the lives and

customs, the ambitions and struggles of men who lived over the summit of the Blue Ridge and beyond the foot-hills of the Cumberlands.

But he was wise enough to know there were many things he did not know. He was brave enough to frankly admit them. When placed in a situation that was new to him, he would try quietly to think his way out of it; and through inheritance and training he thought calmly. He had the mental power to stand at ease under any condition and await sufficient developments to justify him to speak or act. Even German bullets could not hurry nor disconcert him.

He was keenly observant of all that went on around him in the training-camp. Few sounds or motions escaped him, though it was in a seemingly stoic mien that he contemplated the things that were new to him. In the presence of those whose knowledge or training he recognized as superior to his own he calmly waited for them to act, and so accurate were his observations that the officers of his regiment looked upon him as one by nature a soldier, and they said of him that he "always seemed instinctively to know the right thing to do."

Placed at his first banquet board—the guest of honor—with a row of silver by his plate so different from the table service in his humble home, he did not misuse a piece from among them or select one in error. But throughout the courses he was not the first to pick up a needed piece.

His ability to think clearly and quickly, under conditions that tried both heart and brain, was shown in the fight in the Argonne. With eight men, not twenty yards away, charging him with bayonets, he calmly decided to shoot the last man first, and to continue this policy in selecting his mark, so that those remaining would "not see their comrades falling and in panic stop and fire a volley at him."

Military critics analyzing the tactics York used in this fight have been able to find no superior way for removing the menace of the German machine guns that were over the crest of the hill and between him and his regiment, than to form the prisoners he had captured in a column, put the officers in front and march directly to each machine gun-nest, compelling the German officers to order the gunners to surrender and to take their place in line.

Calm and self-controlled, with hair of copper-red and face and neck browned and furrowed by the sun and mountain winds, enured to hardships and ready for them, this young mountaineer moved among his new-found companions at Camp Gordon. Reticent he seemed, but his answer to an inquiry was direct, and his quiet blue-eyes never shifted from the eyes of the man who addressed him. As friendships were formed, his moods were noted by his comrades. At times he was playful as a boy, using cautiously, even gently, the strength he possessed. Then again he would remain, in the midst of the sports, thoughtful, and as tho he were troubled.

Back in the mountains he had but little opportunity to attend school, and his sentences were framed in the quaint construction of his people, and nearly all of them were ungrammatical. There were many who would have regarded him as ignorant. By the standards that hold that education is enlightenment that comes from acquaintance with books and that wisdom is a knowledge of the ways of the world, he was. But he had a training that is rare; advantages that come to too few.

From his father he inherited physical courage; from his mother, moral courage. And both of them spent their lives developing these qualities of manhood in their boy. His father hiked him through the mountains on hunts that would have stoutened the heart of any man to have kept the pace. And he never tolerated the least evidence of fear of man or beast. He taught his boy to so live that he owed apology or explanation to no man.

While I was at Pall Mall, one of his neighbors, speaking of Alvin, said:

"Even as a boy he had his say and did his do, and never stopped to explain a statement or tell what prompted an act. Left those to stand for themselves."

And the little mother, whose frail body was worn from hard work and wracked by the birth of eleven children, was before him the embodiment of gentleness, spirit and faith. When he came from the hunt into the door of that cabin home and hung his gun above the mantel, or came in from the fields where the work was physical, he put from him all feeling of the possession of strength. When he was with her, he was as gentle as the mother herself.

She, too, wanted her son to live in such a way that he would not fear any man. But she wanted his course through life to be over the path her Bible pointed out, so that he would not have the impulse to do those deeds that called for explanation or demanded apology.

From her he inherited those qualities of mind that gave him at all times the full possession of himself. Her simple, home-made philosophy was ever urging her boy to "think clear through" whatever proposition was before him, and when in a situation where those around him were excited "to slow down on what he was doing, and think fast." I have heard her say:

"There hain't no good in gitting excited; you can't do what you ought to do."

She had not seen a railroad-train until she went to the capital of Tennessee to the presentation of the medal of honor given her son by the people of the state. She came upon the platform of the Tabernacle at Nashville wearing the sunbonnet of stays she wore to church in the "Valley of the Three Forks o' the Wolf." The Governor in greeting her, lifted off the sunbonnet. His possession was momentary, for Mrs. York recaptured it in true York style. Her smiling face and nodding head told that the Governor had capitulated. It was pantomime, for the thousands were on their feet waving to her and cheering her. Calm and still smiling, she looked over the demonstration in the vast auditorium more as a spectator than as the cause of the outburst of applause. Later, at the reception at the Governor's mansion, guests gathered around her and she held a levee that crowded one of the big drawing-rooms. Those who sought to measure wit with her found her never at a loss for a reply, and woven through her responses were many similes drawn from her mountain life.

Under her proctorship the moral courage of her son had developed. In her code of manhood there was no tolerance for infirmity of purpose, and mental fear was as degrading and as disintegrating as physical cowardice. He had been a man of the world in the miniature world that the miles of mountains had enclosed around him. He had lived every phase of the life of his people, and lived them openly. When he renounced drinking and gambling he was through with them for all time. When he joined the church, his religion was made the large part of the new plan of his life.

It was while at Camp Gordon that he reconciled his religious convictions with his patriotic duty to his country.

The rugged manhood within him had made him refuse to ask exemption from service and danger on the ground that the doctrine of his church opposed war. But his conscience was troubled that he was deliberately on the mission to kill his fellow man. It was these thoughts that caused his companions to note his moody silences.

In behalf of his mother, who, with many mothers of the land, was bravely trying to still her heart with the thought that her son was on an errand of mercy, the pastor of the church in the valley made out the strongest case he could for Alvin's exemption, and sent it to the officers of his regiment.

Lieut. Col. Edward Buxton, Jr., and Maj.

E. C. B. Danford, who was then the captain of York's company, sent for him. They explained the conditions under which it were possible, if he chose, to secure exemption. They pointed out the way he could remain in the service of his country and not be among the combat troops. The sincerity, the earnestness of York impressed the officers, and they had not one but a number of talks in which the Scriptures were quoted to show the Savior's teachings "when man seeth the sword come upon the land." They brought out many facts about the war that the Tennessee mountaineer had not known.

York did not take the release that lay within his grasp. Instead, he thumbed his Bible in search of passages that justified the use of force.

One day, before the regiment sailed for France, when York's company was leaving the drill-field, Capt. Danford sent for him.

Together they went over many passages of the Bible which both had found.

"If my kingdom were of this world, then would my servants fight."

They were together several hours. At last York said:

"All right; I'm satisfied."

After that there was no reference to religious objection. From the first he had seen the justice of the war. He now saw the righteousness of it.

York's abilities as a soldier were soon revealed. He quickly qualified as a sharpshooter, both as skirmisher and from the top of the trench. In battalion contest formation, where the soldiers run and fall and fire, "shooting at moving targets," it was not difficult for him to score eight hits out of ten shots, and, with a rifle that was new to him. This, too, over a range that began at 600 yards and went down to 100 yards, with the targets in the shape of the head and shoulders of a man. In these maneuvers he attracted the attention of his officers.

The impressive figure of the man with its ever present evidence of reserve force, the strength of his personality, uneducated as he was, made him a natural leader of the men around him. Officers of the regiment have said that he would have received a promotion while in the training-camp but for the policy of not placing in command a man who might be a conscientious objector.

The "All America" Division passed through England on its way to France and the first real fighting they had was in the St. Mihiel Salient. From there they went to the Argonne Forest, where the division was on the front line of the battle for twenty-six days and nights without relief.

It was in the St. Mihiel Salient that York was made a Corporal, and when he came out of the Argonne Forest he was a Sergeant. The armistice was signed a fortnight later.

The war made York more deeply religious. The diary he kept passed from simple notations about "places he had been" to a record of his thoughts and feelings. In it are many quotations from the Bible; many texts of sermons he heard while on the battlefields of France. With the texts were brief notes that would recall the sermons to his memory. The book is really "a history" of his religious development.

When he would kneel by a dying soldier he would record in his diary the talk he had with his comrade and would write the passages of Scripture that he or the dying man had spoken. It was upon this his interests centered. To others he left the task of telling of the battle's result.

He wrote in his diary this simple story

of his fight with the battalion of German machine guns:

"On the 7th day of October we lay in some little holes on the roadside all day. That night we went out and stayed a little while and came back to our holes, the shells bursting all around us. I saw men just blown up by the big German shells which were bursting all around us.

"So the order came for us to take Hill 223 and 240 the 8th.

"So the morning of the 8th just before daylight, we started for the hill at Chatel Chehery. Before we got there it got light and the Germans sent over a heavy barrage and also gas and we put on our gas-masks and just pressed right on through those shells and got to the top of Hill 223 to where we were to start over at 6:10 A.M.

"They were to give us a barrage. The

time came and no barrage, and we had to go without one. So we started over the top at 6:10 A.M. and the Germans were putting their machine guns to working all over the hill in front of us and on our left and right. I was in support and I could see my pals getting picked off until it almost looked like there was none left.

"So 17 of us boys went around on the left flank to see if we couldn't put those guns out of action.

"So when we went around and fell in behind those guns we first saw two Germans with Red Cross band on their arms.

"Some one of the boys shot at them and they ran back to our right.

"So we all ran after them, and when we jumped across a little stream of water that was there, there was about 15 or 20 Germans jumped up and threw up their hands and said, 'Comrade.' The one in charge of us boys told us not to shoot, they were going to give up anyway.

"By this time the Germans from on the hill was shooting at me. Well I was giving them the best I had.

"The Germans had got their machine guns turned around.

"They killed 6 and wounded 3. That just left 8 and then we got into it right. So we had a hard battle for a little while.

"I got hold of a German major and he told me if I wouldn't kill any more of them he would make them quit firing.

"So I told him all right. If he would do it now.

"So he blew a little whistle and they quit shooting and came down and gave up. I had about 80 or 90 Germans there.

"They disarmed and we had another line of Germans to go through to get out. So I called for my men and one answered me from behind a big oak tree and the other men were on my right in the brush.

"So I said, 'Let's get these Germans out of here.' One of my men said, 'It's impossible.' So I said, 'No, let's get them out of here.'

"When my men said that this German major said, 'How many have you got?'

"And I said, 'I got a plenty,' and pointed my pistol at him all the time.

"In this battle I was using a rifle or a 45 Colt automatic pistol.

"So I lined the Germans up in a line of twos and I got between the ones in front and I had the German major before me. So I marched them right straight into those other machine guns, and I got them. When I got back to my Major's P. C. I had 132 prisoners.

"So you can see here in this case of mine where God helped me out. I had been living for God and working in church work sometime before I came to the army. I am a witness to the fact that God did help me out of that hard battle for the bushes were shot off all around me and I never got a scrach.

"So you can see that God will be with you if you will only trust Him, and I say He did save me."

"By this time," he wrote, "the Germans from on the hill was shooting at me. Well, I was giving them the best I had."

That best was the courage to stand his ground and fight it out with them, regardless of their number, for they were the defilers of civilization, murderers of men, the enemies of fair play who had shown no quarter to his pals who were slain unwarned while in the act of granting mercy to men in their power.

That best was the morale of the soldier who believes that justice is on his side and that the justness of God will shield him from harm.

And in physical qualities, it included a heart that was stout and a brain that was clear—a mind that did not weaken when all the hilltop above flashed in a hostile blaze, when the hillside rattled with the death drum-beat of machine gun-fire and while the very air around him was filled with darting lead. As he fought, his mind visualized the tactics of the enemy in the moves they made, and whether the attack upon him was with rifle or machine gun, hand-grenade or bayonet, he met it with an unfailing marksmanship that equalized the disparity in numbers.

Another passage in his direct and simple story shows the character of this man who came from a distant recess of the mountains

with no code of ethics except a confidence in
his fellow man.

Those of the Americans who were not
killed or wounded in the first machine gun-
fire had saved themselves as York had done.
They had dived into the brush and lay flat
upon the ground, behind trees, among the
prisoners, protected by any obstruction they
could find, and the stream of bullets passed
over them.

York was at the left, beyond the edge of
the thicket. The others were shut off by the
underbrush from a view of the German machine guns that were firing on them. York
had the open of the slope of the hill, and it
fell to him to fight the fight. He wrote in
his diary when he could find time, and the
story was written in "fox-holes" in the
Forest of Argonne, in the evenings after the
American soldiers had dug in. Tho his records were for no one but himself, he had no

thought that raised his performance of duty above that of his comrades:

"They killed 6 and wounded 3. That just left 8 and we got into it right. So we had a hard battle for a little while."

Yet, in the height of the fight, not a shot was fired but by York.

In their admiration for him and his remarkable achievement, so that the honor should rest where it belonged, the members of the American patrol who were the survivors of the fight made affidavits that accounted for all of them who were not killed or wounded, and showed the part each took. These affidavits are among the records of Lieut. Col. G. Edward Buxton, Jr., Official Historian of the Eighty-Second Division. At the time of the fight Sergeant York was still a Corporal.

From the affidavit by Private Patrick Donohue:

"During the shooting, I was guarding the mass of Germans taken prisoners and devoted my attention to watching them. When we first came in on the Germans, I fired a shot at them before they surrendered. Afterwards I was busy guarding the prisoners and did not shoot. I could only see Privates Wills, Sacina and Sok. They were also guarding prisoners as I was doing."

From the affidavit by Private Michael A. Sacina:

"I was guarding the prisoners with my rifle and bayonet on the right flank of the group of prisoners. I was so close to these prisoners that the machine gunners could not shoot at me without hitting their own men. This I think saved me from being hit. During the firing, I remained on guard watching these prisoners and unable to turn around and fire myself for this reason. I could not see any of the other men in my detachment. From this point I saw the German captain and had aimed my rifle at him when he blew his whistle for the Germans to stop firing. I saw Corporal York, who called out to us, and when we all joined him, I saw seven Americans beside myself. These were Corp. York, Privates Beardsley, Donohue, Wills, Sok, Johnson and Konotski."

From the affidavit by Private Percy Beardsley:

"I was at first near Corp. York, but soon after thought it would be better to take to cover behind a large tree about fifteen paces in rear of Corp. York. Privates Dymowski and Waring were on each side of me and both were killed by machine gun-fire. I saw Corp. York fire his pistol repeatedly in front of me. I saw Germans who had been hit fall down. I saw the German prisoners who were still in a bunch together waving their hands at the machine gunners on the hill as if motioning for them to go back. Finally the fire stopped and Corp. York told me to have the prisoners fall in columns of two's and take my place in the rear."

From the affidavit by Private George W. Wills:

"When the heavy firing from the machine guns commenced, I was guarding some of the German prisoners. During this time I saw only Privates Donohue, Sacina, Beardsley and Muzzi. Private Swanson was right near me when he was shot. I closed up very close to the Germans with my bayonet on my rifle and prevented some of them who tried to leave the bunch and get into the bushes from leaving. I knew my only chance was to keep them together and also keep them between me and the Germans who were shooting. I heard Corp. York several times shouting to the machine gunners on the hill to come down and surrender, but from where I stood I could not see Corp. York. I saw him, however, when the firing stopped and he told us to get along sides of the column. I formed those near me in columns of two's."

The report which the officers of the Eighty-Second Division made to General Headquarters contained these statements:

"The part which Corporal York individually played in this attack (the capture of the Décauville Railroad) is difficult to estimate. Practically unassisted, he captured 132 Germans (three of whom were officers), took about 35 machine guns and killed no less than 25 of the enemy, later found by others on the scene of York's extraordinary exploit.

"The story has been carefully checked in every possible detail from Headquarters of this Division and is entirely substantiated.

"Altho Corporal York's statement tends to underestimate the desperate odds which he overcame, it has been decided to forward to higher authority the account given in his own words.

"The success of this assault had a far-reaching effect in relieving the enemy pressure against American forces in the heart of the Argonne Forest."

In decorating Sergeant York with the Croix de Guerre with Palm, Marshal Foch said to him:

"What you did was the greatest thing accomplished by any private soldier of all of the armies of Europe."

When the officers of York's regiment were securing the facts for their report to General Headquarters and were recording the stories of the survivors, York was questioned on his efforts to escape the onslaught of the machine guns:

"By this time, those of my men who were left had gotten behind trees, and the men sniped at the Boche. But there wasn't any tree for me, so I just sat in the mud and used my rifle, shooting at the machine gunners."

The officers recall his quaint and memorable answer to the inquiry on the tactics he used to defend himself against the Boche who were in the gun-pits, shooting at him from behind trees and crawling for him through the brush. His method was simple and effective:

"When I seed a German, I jes' tetched him off."

In the afternoon of October 8—York had brought in his prisoners by 10 o'clock in the morning—in the seventeenth hour of that day, the Eighty-Second Division cut the De-cauville Railroad and drove the Germans from it. The pressure against the American forces in the heart of the Argonne Forest was not only relieved, but the advance of the division had aided in the relief of the "Lost Battalion" under the command of the late Col. Whittlesey, which had made its stand in another hollow of those hills only a short distance from the hillside where Sergeant York made his fight.

As the Eighty-Second Division swept up the three hills across the valley from Hill No. 223, the hill on the left—York's Hill—was found cleared of the enemy and there was only the wreckage of the battle that had been fought there.

York's fight occurred on the eighth day of the twenty-eight day and night battle of the Eighty-Second Division in the Argonne. They were in the forest fighting on, when the story went over the world that an American soldier had fought and captured a battalion of German machine gunners.

Even military men doubted its possibility, until the "All America" Division came out of the forest with the records they had made upon the scene, and with the clear exposition of the tactics and the remarkable bravery and generalship that made Sergeant York's achievement possible.

Alvin York faced a new experience. He found himself famous.

This is the end of this publication.

Any remaining blank pages are for our book binding
requirements and are blank on purpose.

To search thousands of interesting publications like this one,
please remember to visit our website at:

http://www.kessinger.net

CPSIA information can be obtained at www.ICGtesting.com
Printed in the USA
BVOW05s1648120115

382956BV00004B/135/A